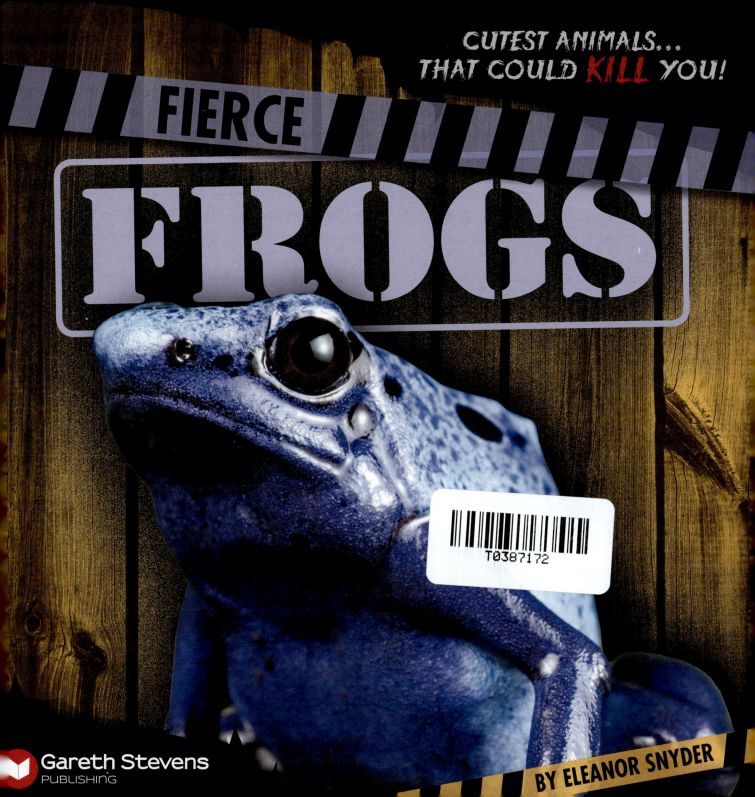

CUTEST ANIMALS...
THAT COULD **KILL** YOU!

FIERCE

FROGS

Gareth Stevens
PUBLISHING

BY ELEANOR SNYDER

T0387172

Please visit our website, www.garethstevens.com. For a free color catalog of all our high-quality books, call toll free 1-800-542-2595 or fax 1-877-542-2596.

Library of Congress Cataloging-in-Publication Data

Names: Snyder, Eleanor, author.
Title: Fierce frogs / Eleanor Snyder.
Description: New York : Gareth Stevens Publishing, [2017] | Series: Cutest
 animals...that could kill you! | Includes bibliographical references and
 index.
Identifiers: LCCN 2016001334 | ISBN 9781482449174 (pbk.) | ISBN 9781482449112 (library bound) |
ISBN 9781482448993 (6 pack)
Subjects: LCSH: Dendrobatidae–Juvenile literature. | Poisonous
 animals–Juvenile literature. | CYAC: Poison frogs.
Classification: LCC QL668.E233 S635 2017 | DDC 597.8/77–dc23
LC record available at http://lccn.loc.gov/2016001334

First Edition

Published in 2017 by
Gareth Stevens Publishing
111 East 14th Street, Suite 349
New York, NY 10003

Copyright © 2017 Gareth Stevens Publishing

Designer: Sarah Liddell
Editor: Therese Shea

Photo credits: Cover, pp. 1, 21 Dirk Ercken/Shutterstock.com; wood texture used throughout Imageman/Shutterstock.com; slash texture used throughout d1sk/Shutterstock.com; p. 5 Klaus Ulrich Mueller/Shutterstock.com; p. 7 Paul Zahl/Contributor/National Geographic/Getty Images; p. 9 Christian Vinces/Shutterstock.com; p. 10 Tamba52/Wikimedia Commons; p. 11 ullstein bild/Contributor/ullstein bild/Getty Images; p. 13 Steve Cooper/Science Source/Getty Images; p. 15 Yves/Wikimedia Commons; p. 17 Joel Sartore/Contributor/National Geographic/Getty Images; p. 19 (dart frog) Skyprayer2005/Shutterstock.com; p. 19 (viper) Robin Moore/National Geographic/Getty Images.

All rights reserved. No part of this book may be reproduced in any form without permission in writing from the publisher, except by a reviewer.

Printed in the United States of America

CPSIA compliance information: Batch #CS16GS: For further information contact Gareth Stevens, New York, New York at 1-800-542-2595.

CONTENTS

Words in the glossary appear in **bold** type the first time they are used in the text.

SO CUTE... AND DEADLY!

Look at the tiny frog on the next page. It's so cute! But don't even think about touching it. Did you know that all frogs are poisonous? While some have poisons that aren't powerful enough to affect people, other frogs are some of the most poisonous creatures on Earth!

Being poisonous is a great **defense** for frogs in the wild, since they have a lot of predators. Many of those animals have learned over time to avoid frogs—or they'll get poisoned.

THE BLUE COLOR OF THIS POISON DART FROG SHOULD TELL YOU TO THINK BEFORE YOU TOUCH IT. BRIGHT COLORS ARE A SIGN OF DANGER IN THE ANIMAL WORLD.

A BIT ABOUT AMPHIBIANS

Frogs are small amphibians. Most begin their life in the water, breaking out of eggs. As tadpoles, they're legless and have a tail. They later grow legs, **absorb** their tail, and begin to look like the land animals we know as frogs. They have smooth, **moist** skin and strong back legs perfect for jumping.

Most frogs are carnivores, or meat eaters. Don't worry—they don't hunt people! They're hungry for bugs, spiders, and worms. Some even eat other frogs or even **reptiles**. But people should be careful of certain species, or kinds, of frogs.

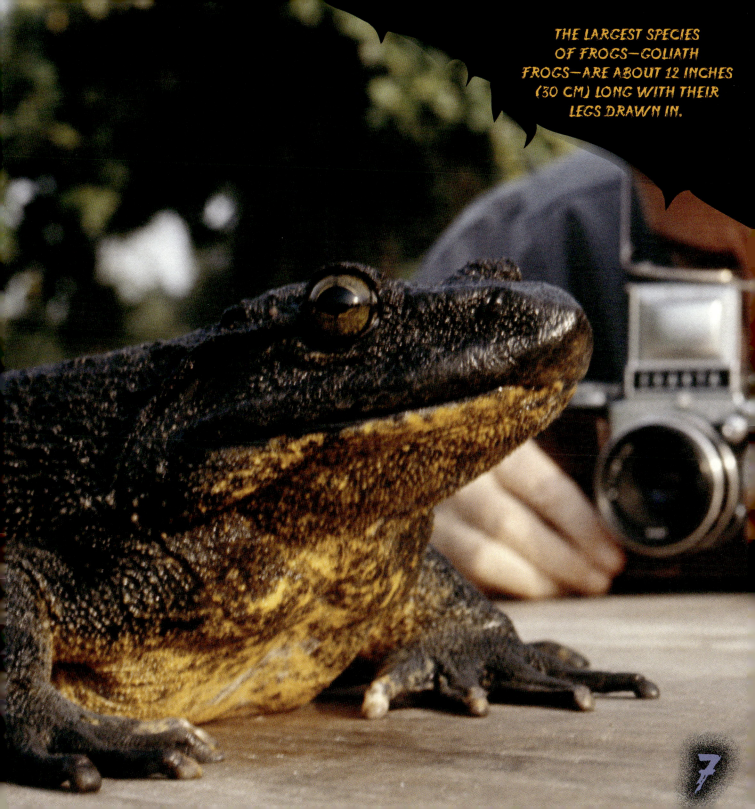

THE LARGEST SPECIES OF FROGS—GOLIATH FROGS—ARE ABOUT 12 INCHES (30 CM) LONG WITH THEIR LEGS DRAWN IN.

POISON FROGS

There are about 180 species of poison dart frogs. They're some of the smallest frogs, sometimes just 1/2 inch (1.3 cm) long.

Poison dart frogs give predators a big clue about their poison—their color. Bright colors in animals tell other animals to stay away. Poison dart frogs can be red, orange, yellow, blue, and bright green. Frogs that are colored to blend in with their surroundings, often duller greens and browns, are usually less toxic.

THE DANGEROUS DETAILS

Three species of poison dart frogs have been found to be deadly to people.

POISON DART FROGS ARE FOUND IN THE FORESTS OF CENTRAL AND SOUTH AMERICA.

GOLDEN POISON DART FROG

Few animals are more poisonous than the golden poison dart frog. Barely 2 inches (5 cm) long, each of these amphibians carries enough poison to kill 10 people! The golden poison dart frog **secretes** its poison through its skin. When an animal bites it or even just touches it, the poison enters their body with deadly results.

In fact, the golden poison dart frog only has one predator that isn't affected by the poison. Scientists think the snake called *Leimadophis epinephelus* built up **immunity** to the poison over time.

LEIMADOPHIS EPINEPHELUS

THE DANGEROUS DETAILS

While golden poison dart frogs are commonly yellow, they can be light green, yellow, orange, or white. They don't have the markings seen on other poison dart frogs.

POISON FROM PLANTS?

Surprisingly, scientists don't think the golden poison dart frog's poison is made in its body. Instead, they think it comes from bugs the frog eats, probably beetles. And they think the beetles get the poison from certain plants they eat.

When golden poison dart frogs are raised in places away from their native **habitat**, they stop secreting poison. In fact, because of their beautiful color, many of these frogs are caught and sold as pets.

THE DANGEROUS DETAILS

The golden poison dart frog's scientific name is Phyllobates terribilis. That even sounds scary!

GOLDEN POISON
DART FROGS EAT BEETLES,
FLIES, CRICKETS,
AND ANTS.

DEADLY DARTS

Natives of Colombia, including the Emberá Indians, used the poisons of the frogs to coat the darts they placed in their blowguns. This practice gave the amphibians their name.

First, they'd heat their darts. Then, they'd wipe the tip of the darts on the back of the frog. The heat caused the frog's back to secrete poison, enough poison to kill a large bird or other small animal. These darts remained poisonous for up to 2 years!

THE DANGEROUS DETAILS

Most frogs are active at night. However, poisonous frogs with bright colors are out during the day. They don't have to hide!

MANY NATIVE PEOPLES OF CENTRAL AND SOUTH AMERICA USED BLOWGUNS TO HUNT SMALL ANIMALS.

HOW IT HARMS

Scientists report that the smallest amount of the golden poison dart frog's poison could kill a human being. How small? Perhaps just 0.0000004 ounce—or even less—is enough. That's about 11 micrograms. While that's a very tiny amount, the tiny frog carries about 1,900 micrograms in all.

The poison contains toxins that attack the human body's **nerves**. It finally causes death by **paralyzing** the **muscles** that help the body breathe and perform other functions.

THE DANGEROUS DETAILS

The golden poison dart frog's poison can enter the human body through the eyes, nose, mouth, or a cut.

A WILD GOLDEN POISON DART FROG COULDN'T BE HANDLED LIKE THIS SAFELY. THIS ONE WAS NOT RAISED IN ITS NATIVE HABITAT.

SCARY SPIKES

It's well-known that there are poisonous frogs, but venomous frogs are a new finding. "Venomous" means the amphibians deliver their poison by biting, jabbing, or stinging. Scientists discovered there are at least two species of frogs that are venomous.

One **herpetologist** learned this the hard way—by being poisoned himself! When he was observing the Brazilian amphibian now called Greening's frog, the frog **injected** venom into his arm through bony spikes on its head. The herpetologist said he felt terrible pain for about 5 hours.

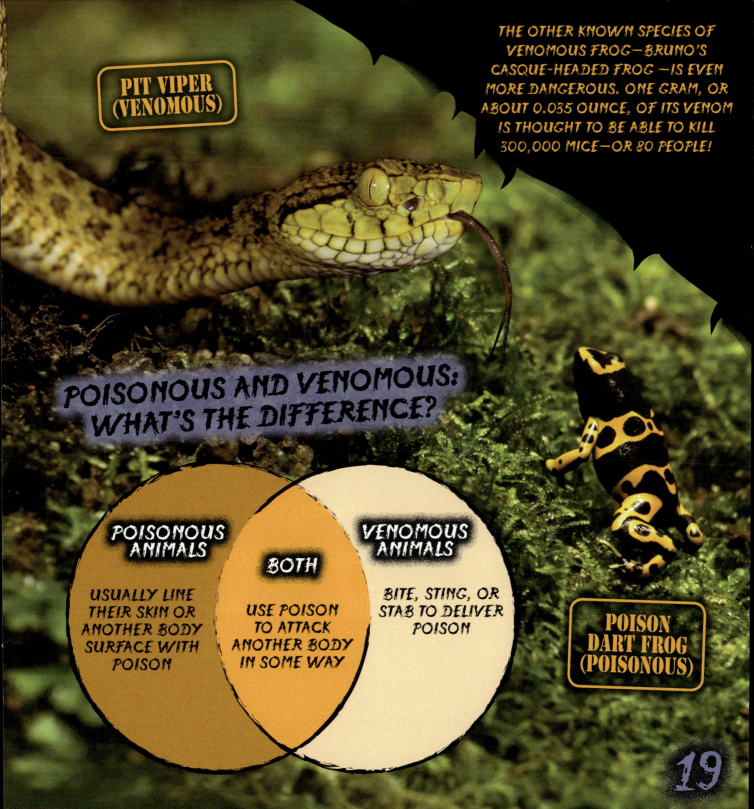

PIT VIPER
(VENOMOUS)

THE OTHER KNOWN SPECIES OF VENOMOUS FROG—BRUNO'S CASQUE-HEADED FROG—IS EVEN MORE DANGEROUS. ONE GRAM, OR ABOUT 0.035 OUNCE, OF ITS VENOM IS THOUGHT TO BE ABLE TO KILL 300,000 MICE—OR 80 PEOPLE!

POISONOUS AND VENOMOUS: WHAT'S THE DIFFERENCE?

POISONOUS ANIMALS
USUALLY LINE THEIR SKIN OR ANOTHER BODY SURFACE WITH POISON

BOTH
USE POISON TO ATTACK ANOTHER BODY IN SOME WAY

VENOMOUS ANIMALS
BITE, STING, OR STAB TO DELIVER POISON

POISON DART FROG
(POISONOUS)

19

FROM TOXINS TO MEDICINES

Strangely, the toxins that are so scary in poison dart frogs may also help save people's lives someday. Scientists are studying them to see if they can be made into **medicines** such as pain-killers. This is one reason why it's important to make sure these cute but deadly creatures don't die out.

Poisonous and venomous frogs don't have many enemies in nature. However, people are their worst enemy, because they cut down frogs' forest habitats. It's up to people to decide: Will these amphibians have a home in the future?

GLOSSARY

absorb: to take into the body

defense: a way of guarding against an enemy

habitat: the natural place where an animal or plant lives

herpetologist: someone who studies reptiles and amphibians

immunity: the condition of being able to withstand something harmful

inject: to use something sharp to force venom into an animal's body

medicine: a drug taken by a sick person to make them well

moist: wet

muscle: one of the parts of the body that allow movement

nerve: a part of the body that sends messages between the brain and the rest of the body

paralyze: to make something lose the ability to move

reptile: an animal that has cold blood, lays eggs, and has a body covered with scales or hard parts

secrete: to produce and release

FOR MORE INFORMATION

BOOKS

Francis, Suzanne, with Jim Breheny. *Dangerous & Deadly Toxic Animals.* New York, NY: Scholastic Inc., 2007.

Mason, Paul. *The World's Most Dangerous Animals.* Chicago, IL: Raintree, 2007.

Raum, Elizabeth. *Poison Dart Frogs.* Mankato, MN: Amicus Ink, 2016.

WEBSITES

Golden Poison Dart Frog
animals.nationalgeographic.com/animals/amphibians/golden-poison-dart-frog/
Read some "fast facts" about this fierce amphibian.

Top 10 Deadly Frogs
animals.mom.me/top-10-deadly-frogs-6776.html
Find out who gets "first prize" for deadliest frog.

Publisher's note to educators and parents: Our editors have carefully reviewed these websites to ensure that they are suitable for students. Many websites change frequently, however, and we cannot guarantee that a site's future contents will continue to meet our high standards of quality and educational value. Be advised that students should be closely supervised whenever they access the Internet.

INDEX